LEAVE A LIGHT ON

LEAVE A LIGHT ON

A Collection of Poems

NIKKI MERRIMAN

CPR Publishing

Copyright © 2023 by Nikki Merriman

All rights reserved. No part of this book may be reproduced in any manner whatsoever without written permission except in the case of brief quotations embodied in critical articles and reviews.

First Printing, 2023

For Amelia.

Preface

Second chances can be glorious, wonderful things. They are rarely deserved but always appreciated. A second chance has the power to change the course of life as we know it. It should come as no surprise that I hold second chances in love in the highest regard; after all, is love not the focus of all the great sonnets? Second chances hold a unique power over us, a power that allows us to right our wrongs, to change our course of action, to turn on our heels and make things right again. Second chances allow us to love where we haven't loved previously, to be better people, and to practice the elusive art of forgiveness.

Leave a Light On focuses on second chances in love and life—second chances that have changed my life in all the best ways. There are moments here where I beg the universe to send a second chance my way, or in the way of someone I love. Some second chances have been small glimmers of hope, some have been large-scale and life-altering, but all have affected my life in wonderful, hopeful, amazing ways.

You never know when the universe is going to throw you a second chance, so keep your heart open.

You have made
a home for yourself
on the tip of my tongue

I still smell your perfume
around every corner of this
godforsakenly beautiful
(haunted)
city
that once witnessed
us falling in love

All I know
is that I'll love you until
my legs give out,
until there's no air left in my lungs,
until my heart beats its very last beat;

In case you ever wonder,
I'm still right here,
glued to the spot
where you told me you loved me
for the very last time

I'm
(s l o w l y)
coming to terms with the fact
that I'm never getting back
her half of my heart

Take me with my humanity,
or do not take me at all

I'll try to take this
one step at a time,
but you know I'll stumble back
every time you tell me
you've missed me

-tell me again

I have no idea what I'm doing
in this crazy life,
but I do know
that I'll keep loving you
every step of the way

I'll fight every day
for whatever love
the universe
decides it is willing to give back to us

They ask me,
"What do you write about?"

How do I explain that,
at any second,
I have at least a thousand ways
to describe the way she looks at me?

Or that
her love
is the only thing
I ever want to write about?

How do I explain the concept
of a muse on fire?

"Write about me,"
you say,
as if every page
in every book I've written
isn't already overflowing with your name

I see your shadow
dance in the morning glow
on the kitchen floor,
and there I go,
falling in love
all over again

And I'd hold your hand
for the world to see

-brave

I watch you let your hair down,
I see it tumble down your back in waves
and think

my god,
what an angel
to be wasted on me

It suddenly makes sense,
in the dark stillness of the night,
that this is it,
you're it

If it had been up to me,
you never would've left.

But then,
I never would've loved *her*.

So I guess what I'm saying,
is that there is a whole version of me
you'll never get to love

but *she* does

They say if you love something,
you should set it free.

So I let you loose to the wind,
and prayed to the stars that the same wind
wouldn't keep you for itself.

I argued with the wind
that day it took you;
I made it promise that
one day,
it would bring you back to me
just as swiftly as it whisked you away.

And here you are,
the most beautiful promise kept.

You are my comforting silence
when the world gets too loud

And here we go,
falling
completely
back in love

-ready, set, go

There's something about this love
I love you with—
it's a love unlike the world
has ever witnessed before

It's in the way
she pulls me closer
in the dead of night,
kissing me as if she were kissing the stars

but in reality,
I'm the one
who's holding the galaxy
in her arms

I tell you I'll love you
for as long as you'll let me,

and then pray to the fates
that you'll decide that it's forever

Falling in love with you
has been but a blur.

a beautiful,
unconditional
blur of forgiveness
and selflessness,
and my god,
so much love.

I pulled another chance
from the depths of the pieces
of my broken heart
and left it on the table next to your keys,
waiting for you to notice it
and pick it up.
Waiting for you to recognize
the bravery and fear it was wrapped in,
for you to hold it in your hands,
look at me,
and say, "welcome home."

We never learned
how to say goodbye
(maybe we weren't supposed to)

You are my truth that I reach for
when the world swirling around us
leaves us questioning everything
we thought we knew.

You are my light
when the night surrounds us
with a darkness so black
we can't find our way out.

You
are everything
to me.

I stand here in front of you
bloody
bruised
scarred
worn
and exhausted,
the dust refusing to settle.

And yet,
I pick up my sword again.

-no surrender

This hope you leave me with,
that you'll be mine again,
has overflowed from my bones
and into my soul—

don't you know
how dangerous
a hope like this can be?

S l o w l y
(but surely)
I stopped writing about you,
about our city,
about the nights we called our own
and the miles between us
(or did I?)

Tell me,
in the dark of the night,
when it's silent and still
and you can hear your heart beating,
does it still beat my name?

Choose me,
here and now,
fully—

or do not choose me at all.

When you walked away,
I left a light on in my heart
in hopes that
someday
maybe
(just maybe)
you'd find your way back home
(and here you are)

Didn't anyone tell you?
Love doesn't break hearts.
(I'm still convinced you're love)

Twenty years from now,
I hope your soul looks back
and longs for mine.

I hope someday you realize
that all along
we've been each other's missing piece.

Tonight is just another night
that I'll whisper your name to the universe
as my head hits the pillow,
wishfully thinking that
once again
you'll be beside me when I wake

So I'll put one foot in front of the other
as my heart still echoes your name,
in hopes that
maybe
this dark,
damp,
unending tunnel
will have even the dimmest light at the end of it

-don't look back now

Let this leaving
be one final act of bravery
(I still don't feel brave)

Show the edges of my shattered heart
how to forget you
(show me how to not love you)

Tell me what to do
when not another soul in the universe
knows mine
like yours does

Tell me what to do
when my soul
is longing
for yours once again

I could look into those deep brown eyes
and tell her I'm falling
back in love with her,
but the truth is,
I never fell out

I'll be forever grateful
for every chance this lifetime has given me
to fall in love
with every part of who you are

No matter how many times
I'm convinced that my heart
has said it all,

It will always have more
to say to you

You shattered my heart,
and I used your
so-called love
as the glue to fix it when you came back.

And then I wondered why
it broke all over again
when that glue didn't stick.

I will pull new words
from places you have not been,
even if I have to invent them myself

-someday

My soul burned for you
like it had never burned before,
and I know yours burned for me too,
but I forgot—

candles always burn uneven

I will hold my own face,
dry my own eyes,
and eventually I will pull myself
from this
ocean
I've cried for you

Maybe all these words
are just about
a single moment in time
between two souls
in this vast eternity

This brand-new beginning
looks a lot to me
like your beautiful face

When our souls crashed into each other
that cold winter night,
the Christmas stars aligned
to light our way through
this universe together

Take my hand,
spin me around,
and never stop dancing
away with my heart

I could've lived with you
in that
one
single
moment
for the rest of eternity

I promise to use my light
to guide you through
your darkest nights,
and when morning finally comes,
I promise to be
by your side
still holding your hand

My heart skips a beat
every time the stars
whisper your name

Maybe
if we're lucky,
this could be something
we want to hold on to
just a little while longer

One day,
love will knock on your door
and you won't remember
that it even left
to begin with

-beginnings

When all is said and done—
when the lights go out
and the door closes—
remember me

You locked your
jaw dropping eyes
on me,
and I knew from that moment on,
my life would never be the same

As this second chance
comes to a close,
I'll close my eyes
and thank the universe
one more time
for the beautiful beginning it once was

And if you turn out to be
a trap,
I will fall
gladly,
willingly
into your arms
over and over again

You may not have brought
much peace to my life
but, my god,
you brought
so
much
love

I tell the skies
of my love for you,
and they weep

You light up my soul
with the brightest shade of gold—
now watch how it shines
only for you

This night sky we're under
is a beautiful showcase
of how even the brightest stars
know how to crumble
with the most magnificent grace

I've been trying to find
a part of me
untouched by you.

I think I might be searching
for something
that can no longer
be found.

Could you do me
one small favor?

Could you fall in love with me
and never look back?

We loved with a love
that will outlive us all;
tell me
how can you walk away
from a force like that?

I trace your skin with mine,
reaching through
to your soul;
everything connecting us
in this moment
lights up with the light of a thousand stars,
and heaven help me,
I think I've fallen in love

Don't you know
I'd unreluctantly go to war
for you?
I'd fight every one
of your demons in the darkness,
in desperate hope that
one day
you'll reach for my hand
instead of the bottle
(I'm reaching)
(Please take it)

My cheeks flush
a shade of pink
they've never been before
as your lips brush against them,
and the butterflies in my heart decide
that they'd like this moment
to stick around
just a bit longer

You buried me alive
with the lies you told,
but by the time you dug me up,
my lungs were too full
of the dirt you forced into them
to breathe you in fully again.

And by the time I coughed up
all your dirt-filled deceit,
and pulled a second chance
from the pits of my scarred-up lungs,
you decided you wanted someone
whose lungs weren't coated
in the soil you sowed.

For me,
there is no gray in love.
There is gold,
there is red,
and sometimes there is blue—
but there is no gray area
in what I feel
in this moment
for you.

This love shines with a beauty
beyond the auroral colors
of the great northern sky,
with the magic
of a universe
not yet discovered,
and an enchantment
incomprehensible
to two beings cursed with something
as finite as the human condition

You kiss me goodnight,
and I can't shake the feeling
of glitter falling from the night sky,
enveloping us in a
quiet
golden
magic
that only comes
when you kiss me like this

When I started writing about her
in 2021,
when the autumn leaves
started to turn
and air was warm
only a few days more,
I never wanted to write her
into a page
filled with anything but infinite love.

I tried to fight her demons
alongside her;
I made them my own,
I danced with them through the flames.

I fell in love with the soul
in which those demons resided,
but when it comes to going
to battle against them,
we have different weapons of choice—

I pick up a pen,
she picks up the bottle.

-wash, rinse, repeat

I roll over at six am,
my tired eyes
locking onto yours,
in an unspoken agreement
that this is where in the universe
we're meant to be

You wrap your arms around me
and I take a deep breath,
breathing you in—
this is love in the flesh

-surrender

There is such joy
in the simplicity
of you wanting to hold my hand

Writing
is a lot like falling in love.
First, you must learn the rules.
Then,
you must
break every one of them
for it to be worth
anything (and everything) at all.

So I'll take a chance
on your Pennsylvanian heart
in hopes that,
when you leave,
you might take my piece of Chicago
with you wherever you land next

I can only pray
that time
will not swallow us whole

When October rolls around,
and it comes time for you
to pack up and move on,
don't forget to pack
my Chicagoan heart
in the front seat of that moving truck.
Bubble Wrap it in our memories,
and keep it safe—
and I promise I'll do the same
for yours.

One touch from your
velvet hands
is all it takes
to make me catch my breath

Sing to me a song
about two people
who beat the odds against them
and loved each other for a lifetime.

Sing to me,
and I'll write for you.

I'll write for you
about two people
who overcame the miles between them and,
you guessed it,
loved each other for a lifetime.

I tried to stitch you up
as you cut your heart open
on your broken bottles,
but they cut me open too.

The alcohol spilled from those bottles
into our lacerated hearts,
burning us both
as I desperately pushed through
to keep stitching,
to keep fighting,
to keep loving.

But it's damn near impossible
to put on a positive face
when you're covered in the
blood and booze
of the woman you love.

So I'll pick up this pen,
flush the alcohol from my burning heart,
stitch myself up,
and reach my hand out to you
in one more (desperate) attempt
to save the life I love so much.

The world was closing in
on our second chance
(this was it)
and somewhere deep down,
we knew we might not get another
(this was the end)
but we were still dancing

-don't let go of me

The violet bruise
of her bottle
is going to be the death of me
(if it doesn't kill her first)

I love the way
his kiss
gets just a little sweeter
every time his lips meet mine

I'm reaching out
my hand to you—
it's holding a chance
at a life
not riddled with intermissions.

Put down the bottle
and take it
(live this life with me).

This is me
giving you the green light
to take me for all that I am
and never let me go

I've spent years
trying to fill
the missing piece of your heart.

But, in order to do that,
you'd have to let me remove
the bottle
you have jammed in there first.

(I'm a much better fit)

And in that moment
I can't help but compare
the broken glass on her floor
to my heart—

shattered,
defenseless from being soaked in her booze,
and crushed, powerless under the weight
of this merciless addiction

My idea of luxury is simple:
you,
soaked in sunlight,
smiling back at me

She stares right through me
with those ghost eyes,
and somewhere behind them
is the same woman
who made me pinky promise
to never leave her
in the middle of this battle.

So I hold her hand
and stroke her hair,
because it may not be her
looking through me with those ghost eyes,
but my god,
she's still so beautiful.

I'll emerge from this war
with more than just the
bruised legs and scraped knees
from my childhood;

I'll emerge
smelling like her booze and perfume,
with a gashed open heart,
covered in her blood and my own.

I'll emerge
black and blue
inside and out,
from the irreversible damage she's caused.

I'll emerge
missing my own life
while fearing for hers,
with no tears left to cry for either.

I'll emerge
still in a constant internal conflict
between trying to save myself,
and turning back to save the love of my life.

I'll love her and miss her
forever
if I emerge at all

-loving an addict

Why didn't anyone tell me?
What a double-edged sword
this second chance
would turn out to be.

Silence hangs
in the space in my soul
that once was yours

I don't know
where life will take you next,
but lately I've been wishing on stars
that it could be the start
of our first adventure together

Tell me something
I don't know about you.

Tell me
you still love me.

Let's tempt fate
and jump off this mountain
we've found ourselves on top of,
hand in hand,
never looking back

Let me into
the unlit corners of your soul;
show me the parts of you
that you hide away from the world
and I will love you more for them

I've chosen love
in every moment with you,
and I'll continue to choose love
for as long as the universe will let me

You kissed me
as the snow fell around us,
and I knew I'd be
helpless
against the pull of your gravity

I kept you like a promise.
It's too bad you can't say the same.

If you cannot hold my hand
in front of other people
the way you do when we're alone,
then do not hold it at all

May we never become
just
familiar strangers

As long as my hand is in yours,
I'll never truly be far from home

You are bringing about
the most beautiful undoing
of everything I thought I knew

I rest my heart
in your soul,
and for the first time in a long time,
I might actually get some sleep

I'm in too deep
for October to come so soon

-stay

Take me home
to your heart
beating against mine,
to your hand
holding my hand,
to our souls intertwined
in the middle of the night

Even my bones
remember how you feel;
they call out your name
in the dead of night

You shuffled in
from the bitter, icy winter,
shook off your coat,
smiled at me,
and I knew in that instant
I'd be defenseless against you

Your listless eyes
stare blankly ahead,
surrounded by half-empty bottles
and the glow of the television,
and for whatever reason,
I find myself searching for
some sliver of hope
in this burning room

I will love you
until the end of time,
until my lungs breathe
their very last breath

-this isn't a poem, this is a prayer

You were never a choice
but I chose you anyway,
and look where we ended up—
tiptoeing through broken fragments
of something that never was
to begin with

Everything I wish I'd said
spills down my cheeks
in salted streams of tears;
what we thought was the beginning
turned out to be the end

Tell me—
did my kisses ever
linger on your skin
the way yours did
on mine?

You'll never see the way
you had me
in a million pieces on the floor
the night you told me you didn't love me

You only loved me
with a bottle in your hand.

I loved you
when the sun rose,
when the sun set,
and in every moment
before and after.

-discrepancies

Your key weighs heavily
on my keychain,
a constant reminder
of a door to a love
we'll never walk through again

It's a special kind of
torture
to be loved with a love
that isn't love at all

Someday,
"goodbye"
will become
"goodnight,"
and all the miles will
dissipate
into nothing but a memory

I guess you were never
mine to begin with,
but, my god,
was I yours

I roll the dice
on a future with you,
and wait with bated breath
for what comes next

I make a list
of what I've kept
and what I've let go,
and I count you in both

You hold me tight
and I can feel my broken bones
slowly
but surely
piecing back together

Love me with a love
that is worth remembering

New plan:
You.
Me.
Forever.

I cannot resist the pull
of your soul's gravity,
so I give in
one last time—
catch me

Nice to meet you—
I think I'll call you
Love

I write countless words,
but at the end,
they all melt together
into your name

You
are my coming home

I can't help but feel
so small
in this vast universe,
but in your love,
I am infinite

I'd follow you
to the ends of the earth
for the chance to hold your hand

You can quiet
the chaos in my soul
with just the touch of your hand

You press your body to mine,
and there I go,
unravelling
at the feeling of you

I catch your eye
from across the kitchen,
and for the first time in ages,
I see
peace
looking back at me

It's so easy
to get lost in your soul;
please,
don't send the search parties
in after me.
Please,
let me stay
just a little while longer.

So I'll pick up this pen
and write our story—
a story of two writers
in the right universe
at the right time—
help me write the ending

If you or someone you know is struggling with addiction, call SAMHSA's National Helpline at
1-800-622-4357

About The Author

Nikki is a runner, dancer, artist, model, and traumatic brain injury survivor from the Chicagoland area. When she isn't writing, she enjoys painting, traveling, baseball, and spending time with her family and pets. More often than not, you can find her on the beach or near the water. There are few things she enjoys more than hearing from her readers; you can find her and more of her work on Instagram @nixwrites_.

www.ingramcontent.com/pod-product-compliance
Lightning Source LLC
Chambersburg PA
CBHW070429010526
44118CB00014B/1972